THE FARMER'S DAY

CHINENYE H.G OFOKANSI

Acknowledgments

I thank God Almighty for His grace so far,

I cannot thank Him enough.

My gratitude also goes to my family, friends and well-wishers, especially my marketers.

Thank you all.

Table of Contents

Acknowledgments iii

CHAPTER ONE... 1

CHAPTER TWO..4

CHAPTER THREE 6

CHAPTER FOUR 9

CHAPTER FIVE 12

CHAPTER SIX 15

CHAPTER SEVEN.. 18

CHAPTER EIGHT 20

CHAPTER NINE 23

CHAPTER TEN 26

CHAPTER ONE

"Do you know what?" Chinedu said to Kosi "I'm sure you don't know how we came to live here. I shall tell you everything. Listen very well because I shall ask you questions.

My father, Mr. Ibeoha, was a farmer in Chief Nwoba's farm, and my mother – Mrs Uzoechi, was a cleaner in the health centre at Mephra. My parents have five children and I am the last. My father worked in Chief Nwoba's farm and plantation. He usually leaves in the morning and comes back in the evening.

He would carry his hoe over his shoulder and his machete in his hand.

My father always comes home sad. I noticed this sadness because whenever he comes home and I go out to meet him, he wouldn't smile to me or touch my head, like my mother always does. And that kept me wondering what I've done wrong.

My mother does go to the hospital early, but she always comes back even before my father leaves for Chief Nwoba's farm. She would come back with dodo and pap, which we use for breakfast before going to school. My father would never join us in the breakfast. He always said he would be late. Later in the evening, he would come back with a long face. So I always think his problem must be hunger.

Questions

1. Who is telling the story? And to who?
2. What were the parents' occupations?
3. What does his father carry to work?
4. What do they use for breakfast?
5. What did Chinedu think made my father always come home sad?

CHAPTER TWO

I always wished there's a way I could help my father's sadness, to make him happy. So whenever he comes back with sad face, I would run to my mother and tell her my father is hungry. But soon I will find out hunger was not my father's problem, and probably not the cause of the sadness. And because I always wished I could help, I found a way of helping him with his hoe or machete, though he always tells me the hoe is heavy for me and the machete might injure me.

On this day, my father came back from Chief Nwoba's plantation. He did not allow me to carry his hoe or machete. He kept the hoe and machete by the wall, in front of our small hut. My mother had finished cooking our dinner, and she told my elder sister, Chidalu, to pour water into a washing basin for our father.

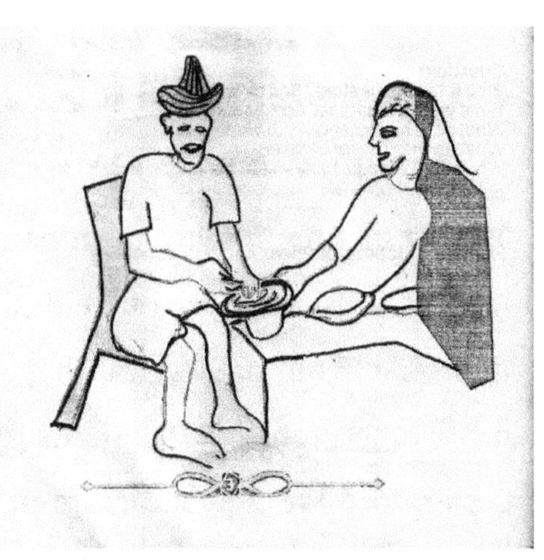

My father washed his hands in the washing basin but he refused to eat, when my mother brought the plates of cocoyam and palm oil for him. I knew very well my father must be hungry. He just reclined on the chair, rested a while before going in to have a night rest.

Questions

1. How did Chinedu try to help his father?
2. Did his father allow him to carry his hoe and machete?
3. What did his father say to him about the hoe and machete?
4. What is his elder sister's name?
5. What did his mother prepare for dinner?

CHAPTER THREE

My mother told us that night that our father was having problems with his work. Nonye, our eldest, asked her what kind of problem our father was having with his work, but our mother refused to tell us. We ate our cocoyam and palm oil. We prayed before we joined our father.

In the morning, our father woke up before all of us. He was already set for his work before we woke up. He surprised me because I thought he wouldn't go to work since he was angry in the night. And unlike other days, he left before our mother came back from the health centre.

I had planned what I would do that day to find out why he was angry, since I didn't go to school. So when my mother did not come back before our father left, it gave me the opportunity to carry out my plans. I trailed behind my father along the bush paths to Chief Nwoba's farm.

I sat on a mound of red earth behind the tall thick green grasses while my father worked with his hoe and machete.

I saw him pull small green grasses off the ground. I saw him harvest the yams from the ground with his hoe. I saw him cut the mature plantains from their stems with his machete. And he packed the plantains in Chief Nwoba's store. Then he made mounds and ridges at a new site on the farm, and watered the farm with the irrigation can. I saw him fell on the ground as he was gathering the farm wastes to burn them. And he soon fell asleep. Then I knew it was time for me to help him because he was tired. I entered Chief Nwoba's farm and continued from where my father stopped. I pulled the weeds off the ground, carried the yams to the barn and was gathering the farm waste to burn them, when I heard a voice that made me freeze like a fish.

Questions

1. How did Chinedu's father surprise him?
2. Why did Chinedu follow his father to work?
3. Where did Chinedu hide as his father worked?
4. When did he take over from his father?
5. What made him freeze like a fish?
6. Find the dictionary meaning of the words "trail" and "opportunity"

CHAPTER FOUR

I knew that voice was not my father's voice. The voice was like a soldier's voice and I knew my father is not a soldier. I thought of running away without looking back to know who it was, but I remembered the soldier might shoot me with his gun. I did not run but slowly, I turned towards my sleeping father, only to find out he has woken from sleep. He was staring in amazement.

"You are sleeping while my farm is being looted?" A huge man I had called a soldier spoke with anger. I had never seen Chief Nwoba but I have heard stories about him. He is very tall. He has big head, and eyes that looked like balls. Mere looking at him would make you afraid because he is a giant. I've heard Mama Nonso who lived in our neighbourhood talk about Chief Nwoba. She said Chief Nwoba was a soldier during the Nigeria civil war. It was then I agreed with her.

"You are here and a thief entered my farm?"

"He is not a thief, Chief" my father said, "He is my son."

"That he is your son does not mean he is not a thief. Why must he come into my farm like that? He waited till you fell asleep. I saw him behind the bush."

My father looked at me with angry eyes. I thought he would rush at me and beat me.

"You and your son planned it," Chief Nwoba said, "You have decided to steal from my farm since I did not give you your wage."

My father pleaded with him but Chief Nwoba did not listen to him. He told my father to pick his hoe and machete and leave and never come back.

Questions

1. Whose voice made Chinedu to stop working?

2.   What did Chief Nwoba say Chinedu came to do
     in his farm? Why did he say so?

3.   Who said Chief Nwoba was a soldier?

4.   What would make one afraid of Chief Nwoba?

5.   What did Chief Nwoba tell Chinedu's father to
     do?

Word Study

Neighbourhood, looted, soldier, huge, civil war.

CHAPTER FIVE

I wished I could tell the ground to open and swallow me. I wished I could tell the wind to carry me away. I left Chief Nwoba's garden immediately. I would have gone to Meche's house to escape my father. Meche is my friend and classmate. We are age mates and schooled at Kaodili Primary School. I knew my father would cut my neck with his machete if he didn't meet me at home.

When I got to our compound, I hid behind the hut. I soon heard my father shouting my name as he approached our compound. I became so afraid that I wanted to urinate in my shorts. So I ran to our open-roof bathroom. My father shouted my name till he entered our hut. I heard my mother telling him that I had been behind the hut. She was begging him to calm down.

"What has Chinedu done?" My mother asked him.

"Why is it that your children don't have ears? Why can't they make use of their ears?" My father asked. "Chinedu followed me to the plantation and got me sacked."

I wanted to rush out from my hiding to explain why I followed him to the farm, but fear did not allow me to come out. I stayed in my hiding throughout that afternoon. Although I was hungry, I did not come out. My mother told my siblings to search for me. They went to Meche's house but I was not there.

Towards evening, my mother came to ease herself near the bathroom and saw me there.

Questions

1. Where could Chinedu have gone to escape his father?
2. What is the name of Chinedu's school?
3. Where did Chinedu hide in their compound?
4. Where did his siblings go looking for him?

5. Who found Chinedu in his hiding?

Word Study

1. Look up and study the following words.

Hiding, siblings, escape, plantation, approached, schooled.

2. Write out the verbs in the present tense

3. Write out the nouns.

CHAPTER SIX

My mother was very surprised when she saw me hiding near the bathroom.

"So you are here and we were looking for you everywhere!"

She dragged me by the ear into our hut. Our father was resting on a raffia mat. He rose immediately he saw me and started scolding me. My mother ordered me to kneel down. I knelt down throughout that afternoon. Our mother later gave me food but tears didn't allow me to enjoy my meal.

In the night my father called all of us and told us that Chief Nwoba has sacked him and our school fees would be difficult to pay. My mother promised to pay the school fees of my siblings. She said she might not be able to pay my school fees.

Meche came to call me the next morning while he was going to school. I told him my parents have not given me my school fees and our teacher would not allow me to enter the classroom. The other day, I did not go to school because of the school fees. That was the day I followed our father to Chief Nwoba's farm.

I didn't go to school that day Meche came and my father didn't go out, but my mother went to clean the health centre. My siblings were not around because they had all gone to school. I was the only one in the primary.

My mother didn't come back early from work as she used to. But when she came back, she was carrying a bag, and I knew she went to the market.

I ran to help her carry the bag. I carried the bag on my head and when we came into our hut, she helped me to carry it down. Inside the bag were foodstuffs – rice, beans, yam and tomatoes. My mother told me she bought cake for me. So I searched the bag for my cake. I took the cake into the room where my mother was. I entered the room and saw my mother counting some money she brought out from her purse. I was happy because I thought God has provided my school fees.

Questions

1. What did Chinedu's mother do when she found him near the bathroom?
2. Where was his father resting when his mother found him?
3. Why did his father call them in the night?
4. Did Chinedu's mother promise to pay his school fees?
5. Name the things in the bag Chinedu's mother brought home from the market.

Word study

Look up and study the following words.

Dragged, immediately, raffia, mat, scolding, promised, foodstuffs, arrived.

CHAPTER SEVEN

My happiness did not last long because the next morning, I found out the money was for Nonye's WAEC. And so that day I didn't go to school again. My mother told me when I was crying that her salary was not enough for Nonye's WAEC. She told me her friend in the office lent her some money to complete it. But no matter what she said that morning, I could not understand why I had to pay the price, why I had to be the sacrificial lamb for Nonye's WAEC. I thought maybe it was because I caused our father to lose his job.

In the afternoon, I refused to eat the rice and stew our mother prepared, although I didn't eat in the morning.

My mother tried to convince me to eat. She said I might fall sick if I continued to reject my food.

I didn't only stop taking my meals; I also stopped doing my home chores. I stopped washing plates which was the work my mother assigned me to do every morning. I thought that was the only way to let them know I was not happy. All these however didn't help, because they didn't give me my school fees the next day.

Questions

1. Who did Chinedu's mother give the money he saw her counting?
2. What did Chinedu do to show his parents he was angry?
3. What did their mother prepare in the afternoon?
4. Who lent Mrs. Uzoechi some money?

Word Study

Happiness, office, salary, convince, lent, sacrificial, price, lamb.

CHAPTER EIGHT

When it obvious to me that all my protest will not help me, I decided to resume my duties in the house. My parents showed surprise when one morning, I woke up early and carried our used plates to where I used to wash them. I went to our metal drum and found there was no water there. I didn't waste time to carry our small plastic gallon to fetch water from the village tap, though fetching water was not my work. Fetching of water was Chidalu's work.

My father came out while I was washing the plates. He stood a while looking at me before going to the front of our compound. When my siblings saw me washing the plates, they wanted to make jest of me but my mother scolded them and told them to face their work.

In the afternoon, when my father came to the rear of our compound, behind our hut with his hoe and machete and began to clear the small acre of land, I said in my mind that he wanted to farm our land, though I imagined how small the farm produce would be, because the land was so small.

Questions

1. What did Chinedu's father do when he saw him washing the plates?
2. What did Chinedu's siblings do when they saw him washing the plates?
3. What did his father do in the afternoon?
4. What did Chinedu think about their land?

Word Study

Obvious, resume, scolded, imagined, acre, jest.

CHAPTER NINE

I didn't go to school that day and because I was not doing any work that afternoon, I decided to join my father in his work on the farm. My father told me I shouldn't bother myself, but I hesitated. I knew he was right because he could finish clearing the land alone without getting tired. I got a smaller machete from our hut and joined my father on the land. He did not stop me from working with him, but he gazed at me for some seconds and continued clearing the grasses.

I used all my strength to cut the grasses. They were strong and tough and the roots were deep-rooted. Sometimes, I had to use the machete to dig up their roots because I didn't have a hoe. My father was making use of his hoe, and the hoe was too big for me.

At a point, while I was trying to dig up the root of some grass I had cut, my machete struck something hard like a stone. I looked closer and saw it was a small shiny glass. My father looked up, asking me what happened. I picked the glass and there were other glasses there too, and an old bag.

I took the small glasses to my father. He looked at them in his palm. He dropped his hoe and entered our hut.

I didn't join him because I thought he was tired of working. I continued working. I came around the old dirty bag again. I picked it up and looked into it and saw more of those glasses.

Questions

1. Why did Chinedu join his father to work?
2. Did Chinedu's father want him to work with him?
3. Why did Chinedu dig the grass roots with his machete?
4. What did he find when he was digging the roots?
5. Was Chinedu's father tired of the work?

Word Study

Obvious, resume, hesitated, tough, struck, deep-rooted.

CHAPTER TEN

My mother came back as I took the bag to our father in the hut. My parents entered their room with the bag. I saw them examining the glasses. My siblings came back soon after and I told them what happened. We sat in front of our hut thinking about the glasses. Next, we saw our mother come out with her black handbag and left.

In the night, when our mother had come back and after we took beans and plantain for dinner, our parents called us together. Our father spoke with joy but he was shedding tears at the same time. He told us God has answered our prayers.

"Chinedu has brought us fortune," he said. "He dug up diamonds from our farm."

Our father said our mother has kept them in a place of safety. My father hugged me and my mother kissed my forehead,

The next day, my father was called by the bank manager of the place where our mother has kept the diamonds. He came back with the news that a rich man wanted to buy the diamonds. My father wanted to know who the rich man was because he thought it might be Chief Nwoba, and he wouldn't like to sell the diamonds to him. So, after one week my father got another call that five rich men wanted to buy the diamonds. Two of them came to our compound that day. My father raised the price when the second chief came. The chief couldn't buy the diamonds at the price my father told him.

The next day, in the evening, Chief Nwoba came to our hut, pleading with my father to sell the diamonds to him.

"Today is my day," My father told him, "Other days are yours. I will not sell the diamonds to you."

"Sell me the diamonds," Chief Nwoba said, "and I shall pay you all I owe you."

My father did not listen to him. He left our compound without my father's response.

It was my mother who pleaded with my father. So the next day, when Chief Nwoba came again my father agreed to sell the diamonds to him. I don't know how much they sold the diamonds to Chief Nwoba. All I know is that we moved from our village to this city and bought this house. My parents enrolled me in a new school. We now have more than we need because God blessed us and our parents invested the money for our future.

Questions

1. What did Chinedu pick from their land?
2. What did Mr. Ibeoha say about Chinedu that night?
3. Where did their mother keep the diamonds?
4. How many chiefs wanted to buy the diamonds?
5. How many chiefs came to Mr. Ibeoha's compound?
6. Who bought the diamonds?
7. What did Mr. Ibeoha do with the money he got from the diamonds?

Word Study

Hugged, raised, invested, future, fortune, safety, owe, enrolled

www.ingramcontent.com/pod-product-compliance
Lightning Source LLC
Chambersburg PA
CBHW071504150726

48000CB00006B/2695